Budding
Entrepreneur

*A story to help children
discover entrepreneurship*

Mathew Georghiou

Budding Entrepreneur is a story to help children discover entrepreneurship. *Entrepreneurship is about more than just running a business. Entrepreneurship is a mindset that empowers individuals to take control of their own future and helps them realize personal goals and objectives. It's about freedom, lifestyle, self-confidence, family, community, and more. The entrepreneurial mindset is one of the most meaningful gifts you can give to a child.*

— *Mathew Georghiou*

Produced and published by **MediaSpark Inc**
© MediaSpark Inc, 2012
www.MediaSpark.com

Part of the award-winning **GoVenture**® series of educational games, mobile apps, books, and more.
www.GoVenture.net

Created in Canada
Printed in the United States of America

ISBN-13: 978-1-894353-24-3
ISBN-10: 1-894353-24-2

10 9 8 7 6 5 4 3 2 1
First Edition

Written by Mathew Georghiou

Photos of children by Wendy McElmon

Sophia is 6 years old. She is super smart. And strong, too. She loves dresses and girly things.

Her brother Milo is 3 years old. He is always smiling and loves to dance and play.

Milo makes sounds but does not talk. He uses his hands to tell Sophia what he is thinking.

Sophia remembers their mom saying that Milo is special because he has Down Syndrome. That he has an extra chromosome. Sophia looked for it one day, but could not find it. Sophia figures having an extra something must be good.

Sophia and Milo are orphans. Their mom and dad were lost at sea in a shipwreck. Sophia and Milo were on the ship too. They got separated from their parents as they boarded the life rafts. They can still remember that scary day.

Sophia and Milo were later rescued, but their parents were never found. Sophia and Milo miss their parents a lot.

It has been hard growing up without parents. Sophia has to take care of herself and her little brother. She finds food for them to eat and even changes Milo's diapers. She is a wonderful big sister.

Milo loves combing Sophia's hair and giving her hugs. Milo laughs so much that Sophia thinks his extra chromosome must be one that makes people extra happy.

One day, Sophia and Milo were walking down Charlotte Street and looking in the shop windows.

Sophia saw a beautiful green dress. She said to Milo, "I would love, love, love to wear that dress someday!"

Milo used his hands to say he liked it too.

In the next shop window there was a red tricycle. Milo gasped with excitement. He pointed at the bicycle and said, "Ank! Ank! Ank!"

Sophia knew what that meant. Milo really wanted that tricycle.

But they had no extra money. Just what they had saved to pay for food and shelter. And they had no family to help them. What were they to do?

Sophia was not sad about not having money. She felt rich because she had a wonderful little brother who loved her. And, she was hopeful that some day her parents would be found too.

Several weeks passed. It was a hot day at the park. Sophia and Milo were sitting under the shade of a tree to keep cool. They were watching people as they walked by.

Milo loves watching people. And he loves when people watch him. So, he decided to dance.

Milo is really funny when he dances. He spins around in circles. He stomps his feet. He shakes his head. And he makes funny sounds that sound like "la, la, la" really fast.

A few people stopped to watch Milo. They were smiling and laughing. Milo loved the attention.

That gave Sophia an idea. She asked a friend nearby to keep an eye on Milo. Sophia ran to the grocery store and bought lemons, sugar, and a jug of water. She squeezed the juice from the lemons and mixed everything together to make lemonade. She tasted some but it was too sour. So she added more sugar. Now it was perfect! Sophia spent the last of her savings to buy some cups.

Sophia ran back to where Milo was dancing. She could not believe her eyes. There were 100 people standing and watching Milo dance. Milo had the biggest smile she had ever seen. And, all of those people were standing in the hot sun. They were thirsty!

Sophia started yelling out loud, "Lemonade. Fresh lemonade!" People seemed interested and asked how much it cost. Sophia said, "$1 for a cup." "I will buy some," said a man wearing a hat. "One for me too, please," said a lady in a fancy skirt. "I'll take three for me and my kids," said a tall man with glasses.

Sophia was pouring the lemonade as fast as she could. One man walked up and told Sophia that she and her brother were very good entrepreneurs.

By the time Milo got tired of dancing, Sophia had sold all of the lemonade. Except for one cup that she had saved for her little brother. "Here you go, Milo. This is for you," said Sophia. "You did some wonderful dancing."

Milo gulped down the lemonade so quickly that some of it went up his nose. Milo and Sophia laughed about that.

Milo sat down and Sophia counted their money. They had $27! Wow, she thought. She looked at the receipt from the grocery store. She could see that it cost her $7 to buy the ingredients for the lemonade and cups. That left her a profit of $20. Just enough to buy her green dress and Milo's tricycle. What a great day!

Sophia was proud of herself. Milo was proud of her too. She now understood why the man said they were very good entrepreneurs. They had very little. They used what they had to make people happy. And, they earned rewards for themselves too.

It started to get dark and rainy so Sophia and Milo packed up their stuff. As they started to leave, they heard someone walking up behind them. The person called out, "Hello there! I heard there was a wonderful dancer and some delicious lemonade here. Did I miss it?"

Sophia and Milo both turned to see who it was. Milo's eyes opened wide. Sophia was speechless. It was a woman and she was speechless too. Sophia recognized her. She recognized Sophia and Milo. Everyone started crying. Milo reached out his arms and yelled, "Mama!"

It was their lost mother. They had finally found each other. And it was all by luck. Mom had no idea that it was her children that were dancing and selling lemonade. She just wanted to find out what all the fuss was about. Wow! What a day.

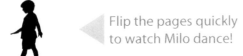

Flip the pages quickly
to watch Milo dance!

The End

(Or is it just the beginning?)

Use these thoughts to discuss entrepreneurship with your child

The reason Sophia and Milo do not have parents is to illustrate that children are capable of taking initiative on their own. Also, many children do not have a typical family support system, so they are more able to relate to such circumstances.

The shipwreck represents a loss of resources and support system. Children may experience significant events in their lives where they feel a sense of loss. The story demonstrates that they can continue to live fulfilling lives after such an event.

The cost and profit numbers offer an opportunity to discuss these concepts in more detail using examples from your own daily life.

Reuniting with their mother at the end of the story represents the children finding that inner flame or champion that helps them realize their full potential. And, that entrepreneurship often rewards you in ways you did not anticipate.

The fate of the father is not mentioned so that the story is left open for imagination and further discovery.

Down Syndrome is a condition where a child is born with an extra chromosome (47 instead of 46). This causes mental and physical delays in how a child develops. Physical features, such as a flat facial profile, eyes with an upward slant, and small mouth and ears, are common. The cause of Down Syndrome is unknown and the effects can vary widely. Despite the challenges, many people with Down Syndrome are able to live happy and productive lives, while enriching the lives of those around them.

Play the **GoVenture Lemonade Stand** simulation and other fun learning games for youth and adults at www.GoVenture.net

CPSIA information can be obtained
at www.ICGtesting.com
Printed in the USA
LVIW021427100413 .:.
328564LV00001B

* 9 7 8 1 8 9 4 3 5 3 2 4 3 *